Bud in the Mud

by Ben Ollie
illustrated by Hector Borlasca

Target Skill Short *Uu*/u/
High-Frequency Words *what, said, was*

PEARSON

Scott
Foresman

Bud is a little pup.

He is a fun little pup.

Jem, Rex, and Jan have fun with Bud.

Bud likes to dig in the mud.

Mom said, "Do not dig in the mud."

But Bud likes to dig.

Jem, Rex, and Jan run and jump.

They run and jump for fun.

Bud digs in the garden.

What was in my garden?

Look at it! Did Bud dig here?

Look at Bud!

We will get the big tub.

Mom will get the suds.

We fill the tub with lots of suds.

Bud fits in the tub.

He tugs at the rags.

We had fun!

Do not dig in the garden, Bud!